Dear Barbara,

I have

presence and

Poetry otherwise –

with best wishes,

Paul

17/8/01

THE GROUND THAT LOVE SEEKS

Even stones have a love,
a love that seeks the ground.

Meister Eckhardt

Leaf tongues
that all Summer long
shaped the wind's will
become for us now
a golden ground

•

I know a golden ground
where poets in candlelight
catch
shadow and flame
from the eyes of the listeners

•

Listen!
There is a ground
beyond sorrow and season
that you
with your golden ears
can open

THE GROUND THAT LOVE SEEKS

Paul Matthews

Paul Matthews

Five Seasons Press
1996

Published in 1996
by Five Seasons Press
Wickton Court, Stoke Prior
Leominster, Herefordshire HR6 0LN

Photoset in 11.5 on 14pt Mergenthaler Sabon
at Five Seasons Press
and printed on Five Seasons recycled paper
by Biddles Ltd
Guildford, Surrey

Cover collage by Ivon Oates

Cover printed by
The Senecio Press, Charlbury

British Library Cataloguing in Publication Data:
A catalogue record for this book
is available from the British Library

ISBN 0 947960 09 0

*This publication has been made possible
through the generosity of a particular Angel*

Acknowledgements

Some of these poems have been published previously in the following magazines:

Poetry Review; Resurgence; The North; The Golden Blade; Theoria to Theory; Folded Sheets; Palantir; Oasis; The Anthroposophical Review; Anthroposophy Today; One; Mugshots; Spectacular Diseases; Outrigger; Chock; Muse; Joe Dimaggio; Horsedealing; Screever; Platform; Profile; Dancing Ledge Mercury; Alembic; Great Works; Lettera; Caduceus.

In the following anthologies:

PEN Anthology 1975, Hutchinson
Transformation: The Poetry of Spiritual Consciousness, Rivelin Grapheme
Poetry in English Now, Blackweir Press
Poetry South East
South West Review
Quademo 3 di Lettera
Pieces of Eight, Driftwood Publications

In the following books and poemsheets:

A Valentine, Cellar Press
Verge, Arc Publications
Opening the Wolf's Skull, Green Horse Publications
A Web of Birdsong Twisted, Share Publications
The Grammar of Darkness, Privately Published
The Fabulous Names of Things, Privately Published
The Gleam, Secret Books
Two Stones, One Bird, Smith/Doorstop Publications
Blank Walls, Aloes Publications
Sing Me The Creation, Hawthorn Press

The versions and titles and groupings published in the present volume supersede all previous ones.

Earlier books by Paul Matthews, not included here, are:

No Other Sun, Exit Publications
To Interpret Love, Privately Published
Descriptions, Driftwood Publications
Footnotes, Writer's Forum
8 Inkblots and Poems, Privately Published
Belladonna, Aquila

Contents

3 · THE GROUND THAT LOVE SEEKS

4 · THE LONG GRASS OF CHILDHOOD

Contents *(continued)*

A Pre Preface for Paul Matthews

Again you question as if to awake from its sleep the matter we keep between us, secret, and pressing for release, and likewise, in this, that other teaching of the gnostics that Spirit is lockt in molecular chains of creation is true—you question my soul to try the lock you have seen in its trembling. But—it is in the orders of the network—the only key is also trembling even as you would hold it steady.

Yet it is not only in this matter of trembling, in this conjunction of the tremendum, that we know *our* spirit. We know that ultimate source of our wondering in the governing intent upon a necessary act, a poem, an embrace, a life-long devotion at work in a house-hold, a steady resolve, in which we see ultimately (as at first we saw) the at-once-radiance-and-in-formation of Christ's passion in the body's suffering to the full its condition.

Yet thruout the strands of the actual fray, break before us, or, to our dismay, are not there. Feeling goes to the extremities of what is and flows thru us from Fountains in that Spiritual World you would question my belief of, from what I find beyond belief. And if they are, as the teaching goes, fountains of our immortal Being, they too, those suns too, must be *burning*, reaching (even as our eyes meet and shy in meeting) beyond reach.

Robert Duncan in London 1968 1973

These words (though not written as such) stand truly as a preface to my work in poetry these twenty years. I cannot claim entirely to understand them, but, reaching beyond reach, I recognize in them a path laid out which, with steady resolve, I have tried to follow.

PM

1

The Grammar of Darkness

In an Oxford Garden

I’ve hung my daughter’s swing
on the appletree. Up she goes,
naked except for her red Wellingtons.

She knows what she wants—
to make the sky turn over;

and I must laugh with her,
not knowing why this walled garden
holds me a moment longer.

.

Clouds change and change,
cast shadows on the wet sheets
flapping on the line.

One moment the bees
drowse in the sun, then a dark
hand drops on the garden.

Suddenly we are sad. Cups empty.
Crumbs on a white plate.

.

Now the same clouds
shift above Oxford colleges.

Up there nothing but future.
Down here the Word   cluttered
with six centuries of History.

But a friend said—
if we read that History aright
we’d know our purpose here.

For Valentine

St John, arriving at his grave, said
love each other. I could say the same
but lack authority;

must say instead   how hard love is.
The word breaks against my teeth.

Sometimes I can love clouds dogs etc
that accept it meekly.

Confronting this Valentine I'm dumb
but think four Winters ago
how we made beeswax candles,
dipping the wick until the wax clung.

So let particulars speak for me—
our little girl shouting *look* those
cats asprawl on the frosty pavement.

Having no candles now we burn snow.
May this love sustain it.

Blank Pages

I

I've stared at this blank page
  half an hour
    anxious
no word of my own
  should smear it.

    Impossible.
A black horse
  bounds into the meadow.
    Well,
when I'm dead the sun
  will bleach it white again.

    The horse
 just stands there
  sniffing the afternoon.
    Burnt rubber
drifting across
  from somebody's bonfire
    maddens him.

He rears against my hand
  as I write this.

2

Scratch this paper

The Names
                    ingrained
might show themselves:

this *Girl*
ripens
within her
whiteness
witness to
many words
but none
her husband

·

this *Deadman*
                    refuses
to close his eyes

there's nothing
    to be afraid of

they merely
                    reflect
the changing aspect
    of the sky

3

Noah's raven still
makes lamentation
over that noose
of waters perched
on a corpse
pecking the eyes out
to and fro
wait long enough
its crooked shadow
would splash
even this paper

4

Whiteness destroys the eye
so we find
blemishes in the paper
to focus on trace
footprints over snow
to find
something familiar a scarecrow
toppled by the frost anything
but this endless whiteness

Grounded in Love

1

and a bee
tapped at

the window while
we were eating.

I distinctly
saw its face.

No place
is holy

unless the one
we stand on

grounded in love.
I was about

to bite an apple
but stopped

with my mouth open.

2

Have you got a garden yet? Ours
is overgrown with honeysuckle.

·

I hope the sea still fills your
bedroom with its rocking.

·

I think the sea is your garden
that doesn't need pruning.

3

(*for Paul Evans*)

Thank you
for telephoning
to say you've won
the poetry prize

I think you
should donate it
to provide some
public drinking fountain

but
if you don't
then buy a balcony
overhanging the sea

and an armchair
where you can hear
not (as I do)
the general roar

but each
particular slap
tap tick
of the water talking

4

My first sight of the Pacific

was when we stopped the car at Limantour Beach
and the baby threw up all over the back seat

So I took an old towel and running to the edge
I was expecting the waves to be six times
the size of English ones but there weren't any

and I dipped the towel into it and I watched
the circles spread

5

My wife's grandfather died in this rocking chair.
This was his house. He built it. Only Kit Carson
reached this valley before him.

The chair squeaks. Not a sad sound. The living
and the dead can rock together sometimes and be
at ease. What's immortal of him

mellows the wood so the chair being empty is empty
specifically of him as though it had just stopped
rocking and could rock again.

Perhaps when he died he was admiring the Navajo
snowshoes on the wall. I'm sure even Kit Carson
abandoned this trail in Winter.

But the dead are narrower and pass easily
with their shadowy merchandise.

6

September 1st. We drove to Gill's Lap.

From the trig point we could see most of the
Ashdown Forest.

The heather was out; a girl galloping her pony
along the sandy path.

The hole in your right shoe let the water in
when you stepped in puddles.

I pointed out the houses of some people I
knew, white among the trees.

It was good to watch them and to know they
didn't know we were watching.

Yeats and Ezra Pound once lived in a cottage at
Coleman's Hatch.

You didn't care.

You said: *September is like after making love,
a quiet satisfaction.*

We heard a paper kite flapping in a Larch tree.

You said you were like a waterfall. I thought
I was like the rain.

And five minutes later a grey drizzle was oblit-
erating the villages and the chequered fields.

At first we stood admiring it. Then we ran away.

Our wet clothes steamed up the inside of the car
making it difficult to drive.

You were wrong about September, and I'm nothing
like the rain.

7

My car with Autumn in its wake winds up
into the forest. When you're 28 years old
it's hard to write poetry.

So switch the engine off, catch some echo
out of silence with the keys still swinging.

And to speak my wife's name—that's hard too,
till watching a damp firework splutter
in the yard we turn to each other again

and laugh quietly.

8

I'm sorry I
spilt bacon fat
on your new
dungarees
but not
sorry enough
to stop
watching this
cracked
yogurt cup
fill up
with rain.

9

When I was shaking out the rugs this evening
I remembered Norman said Mercury and Venus
    are in conjunction

So I went down to the old tennis-court
    to get a good view

Couldn't see any stars but I did find a rusty
bicycle wheel and started rolling it about

The rim was bent   and a sadness   revolving
    between the spokes

Then I threw it too hard and lost it among
    the bushes

10

I met a red dog in the rain

A van forced me to squeeze up against the hedge
and afterwards I couldn't see the dog anymore

So I went on up the lane thinking about my lost
penknife and that with all this rain it must've
rusted away by now

When I reached the new building site I just
stood there watching the rain curve into it

One of the workmen was whistling in a green hut

Then I went home

I found that some rain had dripped through the
ceiling onto my writing desk

One Imaginary Love Poem

I drove into my garage
and switched the engine off.

Noises of rain. Of branches.

Seven years. Unable to find
your face in the driving mirror.

It's what this wind's about.

I could go mad in this dark place
among so many rusting beds.

Because you are dead and I hate
the high talk about it.

A wet dog shaking itself tonight
holds more of Heaven.

There is no Heaven. Unless.
To grapple with. As I do.

Bent across this wheel remembering
how sheer your body was.

Four Imaginary Letters

1

I really like your poem. It just captures that feeling that at any time during the day, even in the most ordinary situation, a deeper level can break through. I had a strange experience of that this morning. When I went into the Baker's shop the door squeaked. And the squeak sounded just like hounds crying. Of course I realized at once it was just the door squeaking, but something in me refuses to believe that and remembers it as hounds. I like the last lines of your poem best:

. . . but when you're asleep
the river brims.

That's great!

2

It's very late now. And it's raining. The girls are asleep. When the rain started I heard their beds creaking, but they didn't wake up. So I can write to you at last. It's good to sit here in the roof angle hearing the rain beat. If it's true the soul wanders in sleep they must be out in it. Their souls drenched. Quite naked. But it's good too sitting here within the small circle of light my lamp casts on the desk. And to think that you lie awake listening to the same rain perhaps.

3

Your funeral today was the procession of each of us into death. Three living generations stalking a dead one.

But you. You seemed just the same. Except that you were dead. Or pretending to be dead. Shut in that silly box.

When we left the cathedral a cold wind was blowing across the steps. The coffin-bearers grabbed frantically at the cloth to keep you to your proper decorum.

But they couldn't disguise that it was you, making some great final gesture of life as the wind bodied it.

And across the street the plane-trees in your old yard were flashing signals—to you, and to anyone whose eyes were right.

Finally the men managed to get you into their car and drove off. When you were alive we never knew what to call you.

4

Sweeping under the bed it made me think of you. How I hid under Mother's bed remember when you and the others couldn't find me.

I heard you counting in the hall. When you came into the bedroom I recognized your ankles. But you didn't look under the bed. So I just stayed there, even after you had all stopped playing.

I remember your voices, anxious in the garden, calling out to me, then growing fainter.

I was watching dust out of sunlight settling there under the bed. I must've been seven. You were much older. One of the big girls.

I could write my name though. Because I wrote it there in the dust. It stuck to my finger. Not dirt, but, like a sediment, filtering out of sleep and quietness.

It was you who found me, wasn't it? After you were all so distraught and anxious, thinking I was lost forever.

You weren't angry though. You slid in beside me. You put your arms round me. Without saying anything. I remember your heart. Beating very fast against my heart.

The Hearth

When Caedmon saw the harp being passed round the fire each in turn to sing (and he couldn't sing) he slipped away, into a barn, and there, cast down in sleep, an angel spoke to him, and when he awoke he wrote down what he remembered.

This was the beginning of English poetry.

When Caedmon slipped away from that fire he withdrew from the old lore. Into a loneliness.

Those fireside stories were a working always within the tribal lore drawn from the hearth that each heart focused on, recognizing itself.

Caedmon had to leave the fireside to receive the new—a Christian poetry, free from magic and the tribe.

But the poems disappoint us. Myth dies into allegory and moralizing. The vision is no longer trusted.

So there is a sadness here. And it continues. Through centuries. Till we long for that hearth folk gathered round. Not just for its warmth, but because fire is the source of stories.

It seems to us now that Caedmon withdrew from hearth and heart into a dark study where the things we love live only by reason of what they stand for. Or as commodities.

I cannot deny an angel guided him. It was our destiny to forget those stories for a time.

But I in my own study here am in despair of it and lonely locked in my English head.

•

But my daughter
(who is four years old)
knows all the stories.
She told us tonight
about a horse of silver leaves
who shook
his riders off and eating snow
inside the forest
he could not die.
And though her heart
(which is mine) rambles
from truth
to nothingness
it is a hearth for us.

The Verge

1

Because it's impossible
that the Rose be spoken
speak
and at the verge unfurl
perpetual crisis
where the heart fails
or that red sustains it.

2

A dying man   come
to the end of speaking
can let his death
speak through him.

Only where death is
can the poem stand
obscene and perfect
stripped of its devices.

3

That some questions are unanswerable
does not mean we shouldn't ask them.

Who created God? How did God create
things out of nothing?

It sounds so childish. We must ask it
anyway, or deny our creaturehood.

A question that makes all men fools.
The mind fails. We fall
into a nothingness. A despair.

But here's the answer:

at this verge where all systems fail
poetry begins. We start imagining.

The Beginning

There were no stars in the beginning.
The sky was a blank eye
seeing nothing.
Skytongue lolling on silence.
Skyhand grasping a web.
It was all window. It was song
of transparent birds unheard
with a great ear thrashing on emptiness.

In the beginning there were no apples
to polish against my sleeve.
It was very still. A still moving.
Moving still. A darkness
filled with the absence of.
An emptiness of apples.

In the beginning I
was not writing this. Your shadow
had never slanted across my stairs.
Nothing to remember then.
Like last Summer I mean
and the children
laughing inside the rainbarrel.

Not even the thought of us?
Not even this question?
What was it then what was it like?
What wasn't it what wasn't it like?
It was a finger listening. Ear
tasting an air of sugarcane.
It was a web of birdsong twisted.

A Green Theology

Leaves catching light
are the true scriptures

I'm freed then
from the need
to describe them

They describe themselves

They are their own
green messages

It is a book
which the wind is turning

Searching a word

Where each man
reads of himself

Reads into it   theologies
of thrush and sparrow

But the tree itself
seems occupied
with a more urgent matter

Look   how it writhes here

This speech turns
always upon itself

Revealed   and veiled again

Where each man reads
(freed from the need to)
a green theology
which the wind is turning

2

The Fabulous Names of Things

The Blue Chair

Start anywhere.
Start with a blue chair.

What is the blue chair
dreaming in the garden?

Thin legs that support
a five mile column of air.

This chair is only its idea
of someone to sit down on it.

A column of birds. The sunlight understands itself
in this blue chair.

Sky-blue. Only a little
solider than the air.

It bruises me, a blue
that fades.

The blue chair gathers
night against its sides.

The night starts there.

The Gleam

I

We've strung a clothesline
here in the deep woods.

Midnight. The firelight
gleams on a towel.

The white towel flaps
under stars and conifers.

Midnight is piled high.
My daughter was afraid of it

but I said don't be   dark
is like a mother.

This wind that comes to us—
why should a child fear

what shares her delight in
playing with a white towel?

Why should I fear it? My bones
cry on the mountainside—

mercy and love dark mother
among the pineboughs.

2

It is your mother when young
standing in a grove of pinetrees.

Water splashes over a stone. The ground
stained orange from an iron spring.

It is a sunlight full of the lonely cries.
You almost saw yourself.

Pretend to be fastening your sleeve
until the danger passes.

3

Opening the Wolf's skull—
it's quiet in there. Clean.
All raging gone.

Three pigeons flying North.
But the thought of her even now
could unravel a rich sleeve.

Not mine though. I can run
my finger along the bone
and still breathe.

4

Blocking my ears to the scream
I saw a dark tree thrashing.

And then a fox crossed the garden
quicker than its name.

I wanted to say the pinebark
has a gleam on it a glimmer of mind

but a squall of smaller words came
worrying the branches.

5

I say the gate
had eyes. I say
its wet rail
gleamed intelligent.

It felt wet. It
certainly was wet
but I had lent
my faculties.

In the wet gate
I was annihilate.
It knew its own
name suddenly.

6

Owls do not agonize.

Having a question
they ask it once

then listen
for the dark to answer.

A Storm of Angels

What right do I have to speak about angels
unless to encounter one in the act of speaking?

It is my birthday. Thundering. I am thirty-one.
The dragon howls at the gate.

What happens on your birthday
foreshadows the whole year.

The ancient battle is enacted   here
in my own yard as the lightning flashes.

And now the rain, that ruster of bicycles,
rides against the window.

We are seeds. We are nothing. Huddled
in the dark armchair. It is a glimpse

of that impossible Michaelmas, where leaves
are more than a falling one by one away.

It is a storm of angels. To wrestle with.
As I do now in trying to speak about them.

The Million Sufferings of the Light

Caroline asked me to write a poem for Advent. *About light and dark,* she said.

So I lift my head. I see branches leaping in wind outside my window. Quick spaces between them where the sun-light flickers through and onto this paper. Quick shapes. Of animals. And of men. For the light has a million faces.

O Caroline, I know nothing about the light. But I love what it plays upon—the light on a heron's back, or cupped in my two hands as I sit here writing this.

The light on my wife's face. A fox's tooth. Rain on an iron gate. Wasps in a jamjar. A tomato sandwich. A white bicycle pump. The Bridge of Sighs. A Meadow Pippit. A small brass key with some writing on it.

These are the million faces between the branches. Invisible light. That longs to be revealed in us. To confront itself. To understand itself in the act of

bending to tie my shoelace. There are times we feel nothing in the Invisible World could compensate for light on a heron's back, or this late afternoon light growing pale across my table.

There are times when all this fury of mating, being born, and dying seems merely a turmoil of wind through branches to articulate the million faces of the light.

Guns and motorbikes and artichokes and emeralds and men and . . . there's never an end of naming. We have lost our way. Unsatisfied. Flickering on this dark wick of things.

The paper is dark now. The wind blowing mad with memories. So dark sometimes, it begins to shine. My wife glances from her book. How our looks give light as well as receive it.

I remember my daughter opening her eyes for the first time. An astonishment. A great shock of light. Never before seen. Never again. As we all are—windows into. Unique articulations of the light.

I remember an old love charm: *Eye-girl lighting a lamp*. As though she kindled it with her eyes. There's a man-light too. We light the Advent candles with our eyes.

And so, as these Winter branches crash against the window, we think of the Child. Alone in his dark stall. As we all are. Only the image of the Child remains. Only here do the million sufferings of the light find a rest and centre. We have lost our way. But here in his two hands the original clay flashes clear out of Eden.

A Welcome

To this hearth which is a heart, welcome.

Welcome to our hearts. Welcome to our breath
        seeking to be song.

May those without a place tonight
        find welcome here.

May those without a tongue be brought to utterance.

Welcome to the stone that has no mouth to cry with.

Welcome to the leaf that trembles on the edge
        of speaking.

Welcome to the owl's high lonely questioning.

May our ears catch answers.

May the Word which hovers above our heads
        find hospitality.

May the song which crosses
between the living and the dead
be part of what we sing.

Welcome to the fabulous Names of things.

Two Streams

Because an old man
said *when you walk*
walk back
the way you came
it's what I'm doing

past the hidden farm
recrossing the
little plank bridge
where two
streams meet

but what he meant
by it isn't apparent
in this landscape
he partakes of now
being dead.

Self Addressed

Don't be misled Paul into thinking poetry begins anywhere else but in The Dentist's Waiting-Room where you sit with two strange women but one goes out when the receptionist says *Mrs Williams please.*

The other just sits there, pretending not to notice this sudden awkward intimacy.

And then she goes out, *Mrs Penfold,* putting her 'Honey' magazine down on the round glass tabletop.

And so you are alone, with the noise of the buses and the soft sound of the dentist's drill that somebody suffers under but it lulls you.

Maybe there is no pain. Or is it that the time has stopped? Pick up the honey that the woman dropped. Poetry begins here.

The Truth of the Story

Yesterday we went to London in a bus.

Iona sat next to me.

She is a handwriting expert, and eats rice
and broccoli out of a plastic tub.

When we reached Whyteleafe I told her
that a friend of mine had once
seen an elf there out of the train window.

Just as I was saying it we passed
an 'Elf' petrol station, and that surely
confirms the truth of the story.

Further up the road
we drew alongside another bus
which was full of our friends,
but they looked rather strange there
as they waved to us with the rain
falling down into the gap between us.

Dr Strange is the name of a teacher
that Iona once had, and maybe my signature
is not as degenerate as it looks.

It might even reveal a few noble qualities.

A Week of Words

Middle names must be good for something. I've got two. *Michael Forster*. I was playing around with them, turning them about, and suddenly there stood Leachim Retsrof himself, cut off by wolves and snow, with the ink frozen in his inkwell.

I thought perhaps I'd make some translations from his immortal works. But I didn't get very far—

Only whose heart
smokes on this anvil
understands
what the kingfisher
bargained for—was all I could manage. It pleases me though that a man's collected works might consist of a single sentence, and his immortality rest thereon.

Then I decided to make a collage of things I overheard or read during one week and call it *A Week of Words*. That didn't come to much either—

He goes everywhere with a bucket full of tiny cars was the first one. Kate wrote it to us in a letter (you won't know her), and later I overheard myself muttering it as I drove to Tunbridge Wells to fetch my daughter's doll from the doll's hospital because its leg had come off.

The second was *Was Christ the first atheist?* which my friend Ricardo (I don't suppose you know him either) asked as we were walking up through the woods after I had given a talk about Nerval's great poem *The Christ in the Olive Grove*. When he said it we both laughed a lot, but quietly because it was serious really and the owls were beginning to hoot from the limetree.

And the last was something I found in the Icelandic Saga of Grettir the Strong—*He was the boldest and most active one-legged man that ever came to Iceland.*

Not Grettir though. He was a two-legged outlaw who kills at least one person on every page but they deserve it. Grettir wasn't afraid of anybody.

But he was afraid of the dark. You don't find men like Thorir Long-Chin, Thord the Yeller, Thorgeir Bottleneck, Ondott Crow or Thorbjorn the Salmonman anymore. And as for Ivar the Boneless I've always imagined him like some human jellyfish without any truth in him.

Was it Confucius who said *the heart itself is a kind of anvil?*

No. It was me.

To Live on the Edge of Things

Walking. Four of us. Down hill. Past the lake. Turn right and into the larchwood (if it's not too muddy) where the man first said *when you walk walk back the way you came*. Said also *there are eyes in the wood*. And this is one of them, dark, but the sun bright at the far edges.

Debbie. She's feeling cold. My shoes. Are getting muddy. And I'm too poor to buy some new ones. *You can wear my jacket if you promise not to read my diary.*

Jump over the barbed wire into a green field and then walk in it where the mud shines purple and black and into the woods again. Looking for the place of conversation.

It is prepared for us. David met his best friend yesterday. No longer best though, *but he coughs in the same old way.*

Talking, talking. An aeroplane roars overhead. The people inside. What they talk about, sealed in a little world that roars through our world in the wood an instant and then out again.

Do you ever play that game? glancing up, catching somebody's eye, glance down again, knowing he knows, he knowing you know, but pretending not to? Yes yes we all laugh because it's true but we never told anyone.

And the old friend I met turned out to be an atheist. Debbie has never been an atheist. She has never even seen one. David hasn't met one for a long time but would like to. And me thinking there may even be one quite near us with his eyes dilating in the dark eye of the wood.

Silence. An aeroplane roars. *This is the noisiest wood I've ever been in*. Let's climb a mountain, take up sky-diving or something—to live on the edge of things like Stephanie's friend does.

To the Lady

Here I am. There
is the grass outside
and the wide sky;

and you are involved somehow.

It's not a vision I ask for.
Something simpler. Some apprehension
of your glance within this green.

You are a woman certainly. I've seen
where you would have been
if I'd looked a moment sooner.

Lady without footprint.

The slight lean of your head
coincides
with how a bough bends
and makes it girlish.

How you laugh the light.

But sometimes I have found you
in the night side of a leaf—
a grief without eyelids.

Lady I would name you in grass and flower
and speak no word about the Spirit.

A Woman Pouring Milk

Thank you Vermeer
for a glimpse of interiors
and a door that opens
into rooms beyond rooms
where a brown light falls

And your Woman Pouring Milk
cares nothing for this
fame you've laid on her
yellow and blue
but she *is* famous
You've caught
what's famous about her

The jug   how
tenderly she holds it

And why shouldn't I
be content that way
with how the light
grazes my shoulder

Yes but this woman's
not even aware
of her own contentment
and I in trying to be so
am always at one remove

Even if I shouted
she would not turn
towards the thought
that she's a beauty looked at

There is bread on her table
and her hands are bread
and her face is bread
and I wish I was bread
and not this thinking thing
always at one remove

I want to be poured
the way she pours herself
out into the mixture

The Incomprehensible Ingredients of Fire

Dear Christopher Smart,

I saw on the map today that Shipbourne where you were born is on the Medway, downstream from where I live in Forest Row. It pleases me to think so. You are dead—I know that. But it's the same river. Why should a simple thing like death keep us from talking?

William Blake called this valley *Beulah*—a soft dreamy place. Impossible to stay here. Maybe even as a child you heard your madness whistling from the thornbrakes. Something beckoning.

Oh I've read how you won those poetry prizes at Cambridge. You could have made quite a career for yourself I suppose, except that you read God's name *in the grain of wood, . . . in the incomprehensible ingredients of fire,* and had to go down on your knees in the presence of it.

They locked you away for that, but could not keep you from your *Jubilate.*

I've been reading that 'mad' poem of yours again. Don't think me just another of those gawpers you complain of. It's true I don't understand it, but I could read whole libraries of books, understand them, and never come to poetry.

But in your book I find the very incomprehensible ingredients of fire you spoke of. All comprehending falls away before this kindling. I mean my eyes look out of the window differently knowing that Sun and Moon are secretly at work there *weaving a garment for us.*

It was a shirt of fire they wove you. How can a man live whose eyes see nothing but the Glory?

The Wound that Keeps Us Alive

(after Mantegna)

Today St Sebastian stands bound to his pillar
transfixed by fifteen arrows, each fatal,
but his blood beats against them all.

The pillar stands among broken statues, flotsam
of a despair from before Christ's coming.

His tormentors hurry from the scene. The saint
forgives them of course, shifting his gaze
inwards to shape clouds into horsemen riding
to a far country.

The wounds to limb and torso are nothing,
but the newly struck shaft between his eyebrows
quivers against Christ who loosed it.

Hard to forgive, this wound that keeps him alive
while everything else crumbles.

The Brooding Place

I'm bored tonight, thumbing the pages
of an old Devotion where the God is *every*
thing that is good, tenderly wrapping us.

I'll write a letter instead: *Dear David,*
how are you managing in all this snow?

This circle of light that my lamp casts
is such a small place to be alive in.

Dear David, God was so bored they say
he hatched a universe to take his mind off it.

So what's the difference between this shell
I languish in and that first brooding place?

Only the will perhaps. I will
to be bored then. This inch
is enough. This airy stuff
suffices to fill it up.

Dear David, size of a hazelnut, any moment
we might suddenly fall into destruction.

The Question

Who are you?
in a turnip field.

No words
but the eyes ask it.

And, scattered
across the hillside,
those other labourers
turn within that
same question.

It's there
inside the sunlight
however we shy
away our eyes.

Who am I
who ask you this?

Naked Light

I am I

You are you

You are not me

I am never you

I look at you

I see your pretty dress
That it sways a little

That your nakedness
takes a shape inside it

I see your eyes

The light there

Yes it hurts me

It betrays all
that your clothes so
carefully hide away

Your whole self brims

I say your whole self
gathers at your eye

And I
would speak to you

And mean to

And I don't know
what I mean

Love-words I want
to meet you

I who am I
who am never you

Please speak to me
Give it a human shape

This naked
light from your eyes

Facing the Light

I
I opened
and the light fell
I faced the open

·

The light fell
My face fell

·

I fell on my face
and and
the I
the open

·

The hatch fell
I fell from light
I feared the open light

·

How lightly I fell

·

I opened my face
The light opened my face
I opened to the face of light

·

Open open
I fell open
I faced my face
The light hatched open

The Dance of Death

Here is your birthday present—
      a copy of Holbein's
            The Dance of Death.

I bought it in spite
      of myself (forgive
            me)   a risk

I had to take.
      I cannot exist
            without creating

tensions between   us
      and that skeleton
            who skips

and cavorts his way
      through these woodcuts.
            Dust to dust you will say

is not a birthday gift.
      Yet here's the evidence:
            Death drives the plough,

and when the sailors abandon hope
      it's Death alone
            who holds the mast up.

Little Girls in Conversation

There's an old story told
        told endlessly   of children
                tossing a golden ball

across
        and across
                weaving a net in air—

their whole hearts
        given and found
                in that parabola.

Little girls in conversation   wise
        before their heads
                are heavy with it.

Held on a single strand.

And then.
        And then one girl
                fumbles it   follows

where it falls
        (an old yarn)
                into the tall grasses.

Do you remember this?
        how the children
                shout in the distance?

And she is lost to them
        groping about
                for something golden.

The clue unwinds from here.

But would we have tossed
        hearts so lightly
                if we had known

this jeopardy?   that the ball
falls into the grass
that the ground

must open
mouthing a syllable
that makes us blush.

The story is told—across
and across—our whole hearts
broken and lost.

And our heads grow heavy with it.

Everything Acts to Further

Into the space of the question
        comes *a shoal of fishes.*
                And there's an answer

in the nets they weave
        which they unwork again
                soon as woven.

I am answered but still in quest
        where the fish, self-lit,
                dart upon darkness.

·

And then *the court ladies* come
        with their 10,000 prescribed graces
                and their 80,000 obediences.

They pause before the fish-tank,
        giggle a little, and chink
                silver bangles. Teeth—

just to laugh with.
        Each of their childhoods
                cramped into tiny slippers.

But when the fish dart so
        that impossible thought
                could almost come to them

to kick their clogs off, and run
        barefoot in the place such
                quick thoughts come from.

3

The Ground that Love Seeks

The Simple Ground

Stones are not fibbers
They are the first-born

We bump up against
this rough brother
and say 'I'

·

Bring sorrow to stone

Let your grief break
wave on wave against
that simple ground

·

Cast down
upon this shore

Maybe I could share
words with a stone

It exactly
fits the hollow

Yes certainly I can
love this thing
so utterly outward

It does allow me
It keeps nothing back

Losing Ground

Now a mist blows in

The fields
dissolve in it

and you
little ten years old
cling
to your mother so

You don't
want ever to die

It is a thought
too big

Let sleep take you

Let the mist
wrap you with its
hundred islands

·

Did St Cuthbert
really pass this way?

We need some geography
to hang our names on

We need a history

Tonight so dark—
guillimot and gull
reclaim the saint's itinerary

Their cry is always
justice in a wave breaking

But there's a mercy on us

But it hurts to hold it
in such a little body

Falling into the Ground

Unless a grain of wheat
fall into the ground and die
it abideth alone
there among the rocks
at St David's Head.

Unless a grain fall
and the rain fall upon that
and a wind shake the ridgepole
we abide each
alone in the long night.

And did we die there
under that great seige of weathers?
lying awake night long
with our minds only
holding the guyropes.

The children slept through it.
But you and I—
we fell into the ground.
We became all ear
for the darkness beating down.

For unless we die there
willing to be wind merely   rain
and rock and a simple fire
we abide each alone
and there is no love in us.

Love's Ground

I knew a cry before the world began.
I know a love that hammers in the stone.
Through rock and flower and flesh and human heart
It labours silently and most alone.

I know a joy that aches within the bone.
I know a hurt that lurks within a smile.
All lovers for their bliss must toss and groan
And on a cry lose loneliness a while.

I know a cry that One between sky and earth
Hung on a cross cried loud and all alone
To call this spoken world back to his Word
And rock and flesh and flower to make at-one.

Love's Fabric

(for Chris and Signe Schaefer
on their departure for the city)

May this tablecloth be spread
first
with your family bread

then a grace come about you
that whenever you shake
crumbs out at the door

the sparrows might carry
sweetness to the sour
salt to the savourless.

Thy cup runneth over
into the unfamiliar
by-ways of the city.

Say simply *tablecloth be spread*
and all hearts
can feast there.

It is love's fabric—
many strands of us
woven together.

The Last Pages

Five minutes after midnight on New Year's Eve, 1980/81, Saturn and Jupiter moved into conjunction. In writing this journal the possible significance of this was my contemplation, together with the understanding that the prophesies of Nostradamus end with the year 1999.

26/12/80

What's knocking?
Maybe some starry thing.

In the dark of the year
the household gathers in.

Our house is prepared, Nostradamus.
Turn your last pages.

27/12/80

The kettle boils. Cold midnight
in the dark of the year.

Those wagging leaves fell away.
And where are the friends I had?

Half way around the Earth.
But I could lean into the silence here

and into theirs. No trouble.
They are closer than sight.

28/12/80

North-West you've gone
into another city.

It is your birthday.
It is the night I was conceived

37 years ago. And I'm not
wise yet.

Each day has its wisdom though.
It lights up the flesh anew.

Skin-wise. Bone-wise.
Take your hat off to a star.

29/12/80

The family opposite has a new dog.
Their teenage daughter likes to play with it.
Shaking its rope she sends a large loop along.
These days between Christmas and Epiphany
  are hidden from the Devil's eye.
He cannot find her.
Words are not words here. There is a hush
  behind them.

•

A white cat leaps to the fence
and sharpens its claws there.

My daughter's violin gives meaning
but what I cannot say.

The bow makes sound what's hidden
there in the wire. Sweet and sad.

It is the pain of the Earth
that sings so sweetly.

30/12/80

We met three wanderers upon the hill—
Heart, and Mind and that other Dark Faculty.
Bless us. We are all unwrought. Not wisdom,
only the myrrh we have. And a dubious star
to guide us.

31/12/80

it blows cold
against my knees
Nostradamus

patter of snow

no malice

pattern of stars
won't harm us

only the wind's
paternoster

raging harmonies

how it blows
Nostradamus cold
in the hedgerows

turn your last pages

Some Inklings

1

Snails leave silver traces.
We leave none.
                                        The air
quite closes upon
                                             the hollows
that our faces filled.
We are utterly
                                      here and gone.

2

I was trying to be all ear in listening
to the rain upon the oakleaves and on the road
and the cars splashing by, and not to exclude them
for being unnatural. They belong to the rhythm—
the swish, the dying away. And the rain dying away.
Then the wind coming and sighing. And is it
my own sigh there? or the world's true sadness?
—a feeling for something lost or gone.

3

Quite mad today I've been.
I wanted to be a tree;
To cast my mind upon the water
And to not be anymore me.

Oh not to die I mean,
But to be unmade rather.
I asked the wind upon the water
To be my father.

4

Midsummer night
the jazz
through the walls
a pink
rose makes me
suddenly weep
yes it keeps on
sending out messages
a pulse an impulse   I'm
getting it rose
it reaches me
what you do
to the light

5

Give up the book
What to read
but sunlight
upon the brook

No vanity
where the brown
wren sips no
angst among grasses

92 million miles
the light
comes searching for you
and now it finds you

What Does Appellation Matter?

Charlotte and Willow and Thel
went down to the Haven, and the boat
with TRIPS written on it soon came in.

It was a blue boat room enough for twelve.
We watched them anxious from the clifftop
as the captain helped them aboard.

Gulls. And waves. And a blue boy shouts
from the quay. And what is the tense of this?
Oh these are enduring things

except that these girls we love
will not be girls one day, but women anxious
as a boat grows smaller, stretching the eyes.

But today. Let today be sufficient to itself
with the girls in a boat without us
and a small rain.

Here at the land's edge, where the rocks
wait without thought (or it's a slow thought),
we have all grown suddenly smaller.

Where are you girls? Gone out of sight.
The seagulls never laugh. It's much
too serious a business.

Now that it's high tide all the little boats
are bobbing with their painted names
that we can't read from here.

Oh here where the land ends
what does appellation matter?

Yet we who watch say Charlotte
and Willow and Thel be given back to us
out of that nonentity.

A Confirmation

(for Thel)

A rainstorm shook the window
when you were born,
but today on your Confirmation
even you might
pausing a moment say
how strange to be this girl I am
under the Flowering Cherry.

A stone is firm.
A purpose in the mind
is firm.
But how can a gust like you
find confirmation   unless
under the flowering tree
you pause
and in the stillness find
God's ground to stand on.

A Reflection

(for Willow)

Mirror, new mirror,
let no false glamour intrude,
no tricks of the quicksilver,
but give me my true face back.

Lend, when I ask for it,
beauty without blemish,
not false, but a possibility
glimpsed from far back.

Treat the light kindly;
and when
from among the flatterers
I return to my room
weary of world-ways
render my childhood back.

A Black Lanthorne

(for Margli)

Every natural body, said Thomas Vaughan,
is a kind of black lanthorne.

How inwardly I feel this candle lit,
streaming deep down dark and seeking exit.

Sometimes when I meet you eye to eye
we catch a gleam deep down to find a way by.

This kindly light indwells each
breathing creature, *but is eclipsed*
with the grossnesse of the matter.

Lucky To Be A Man

Tonight with the moon so full
I'll not deny, but say yes I'm lucky

leaning my dark ear into the shell of night
where the waves are almost speaking.

But they don't speak. But they could speak.
And I try so hard to hear them.

Lucky to be a man. You're even luckier.
Your whole body forever is a wave
    that's breaking.

It makes me laugh and be sad. It makes me
long for a place beyond the almost.

Maybe you live there. Maybe a woman does.
You walk on the beach and know,

and your lover awaits you.

Things

What I'll miss most when I'm dead is
things that the light shines on.
If there aren't wet leaves in Heaven
then almost I don't want to go there.
If there isn't the possibility
of silly particulars
like library cards on a table
then I almost don't want to go there.
Library cards—because here some happen to be.
I am a small Englishman in an infinite Universe
looking at library cards. That's funny.
In fact it frightens me.

·

I am in my room, surrounded by the things
which have somehow clung to my existence;
a picture of squirrels, a desk with inkstains
(it was my grandfather's before me),
a Buddha and a jar of Nivea,
a pottery lion lying among rosepetals.
These are my things. They comfort
and encumber me.

But Buddha, what about you?
Your sides are so sheer.
You gave all your riches away.
And can you still hold
on to yourself as a person?

Did Christ give up his things too?
He had a seamless garment.
The other things came when he needed them,
a coin in a fish's mouth,
ointment for his feet,
a crown of thorns.
Well, he didn't despise things.
He ate bread readily.
He loved the boats of his disciples.

And it's not just things that we love
but one thing next to another—
this African Violet beside the tuning fork,
this pen in my hand
as the rain outside falls among Quinces.
These things have happened before;
but when I happen to be there
and notice the shape of the space between them
then a new thing arises in the Universe.
This was unplanned.
This event without karma.

Angels, though infinitely greater than us,
know nothing of this.
But Christ knows it.
He came for that purpose—
to write on a particular ground
with his little finger.

•

The Gods have enough of immortality
and need things.
They need cuckoos in a Damson tree,
they need Rhubarb flapping beside a gate.
Their paternoster is an honest man
who can hammer a nail straight.

Where Beauty Lies

The Rhododendrons accept
all sadness into themselves
then render it back changed
with a purple glow.

If I could risk that. Love.
And not be shy.
Then I'd walk in the garden
and give sadness away—
to the Chaffinch, to the Gate,
to this bright Laburnum here
so yellow and beautiful,
so beautiful and dangerous.
Ah, that's what I'm on about.
It's risky where beauty lies.

Surely in Spring we dare
like the flowers be beautiful.
They do not shy.
They shout look at me look.
They are wide open.
And we if we do dare
can gaze into the heart of it,
like the bee, into the pollen,
and be covered all over.

And   yes   shall I risk it?
To be plunged in, to be entirely
beautiful in the garden
and along the paths
and into the secret heart
where the Caterpillar
spins in the sunlight
and the Rose
shows no shame at all
for its blatant flowering.

Shall I risk
sharing these words with you?
What if I cried?
You will gaze into the heart of me.
And I am shy
of being seen
to be beautiful.

The Blossom

When the girl in the appletree
says hello to you
you must pause of course
and however important
you thought
that your business was
this business overrides it.

Not that she's your business.
Maybe her beauty
seeks a purpose all its own
among those appleboughs
beyond all thought of fruiting.

Carrying Language into a Wood

Aspen is the noisiest tree. It flares
above the quietness of the wood.

·

The bluebells are over. We six
are the only things not green.

·

Loud flowers we are.
Surely we do intrude
with our brash language.

·

Who tore
off the blackbird's wing?
It has one white feather.
We hurry too fast
past all the messages.

·

No one really enters a wood
unless they are prepared
to give up their language.

·

Be like a tree, Michael.
Logs under the saw
scream in pain.

·

Paula is the very last bluebell
deepening to purple.

·

When language falls away
we see that each leaf
bears a name upon it.

·

This paper was a tree once.
If I dropped it in the wood
it would not be litter.

·

Generations of leaves litter the wood.
Our names enter the dark ground.
I love these six people.

·

We have found our initials carved.
Oh this is the best
corner of the world, Michael.

A Poet in a Shed

I walked down
to see what the gardeners do in Winter.

No one was there.

Looking back I saw that the lights
had come on in the big house.

I took out my pencil and paper
and wrote: *An old toolshed.*
The scarecrow's clothes
are piled here for the Winter.

Then a gun went off. It startled me
in that still place.

Then Esther came along and I was shy
to be a poet in a shed and said
Esther do you mind it?

The girl with the wheelbarrow
gave me permission
to write
these words about her.

The barrow sounded emptier as she trundled off.

It was so silent there. *You too*
could be as full
as a blue rainbarrel.

Through the trees I could see a girl and a door.
It was the house calling me home.

Here on this chopping block
let me rest
my life a while.

The Ground that Love Seeks

(for Francis Edmunds)

December 17th. We gave his ashes
to the ground. The choir sang
and a few words were spoken.

We could hardly hear them though
for the wind kept tossing them
out among the birchboughs.

If we felt small   I say
that a larger breath was lifting
among those ashes as we poured them.

I glanced at the faces. Solemn not sad.
For surely he chose such a day
to be shaking the old branches.

They were faces I had loved
and quarrelled with, but that quarrelling
was only the wind's now.

We stood on the damp ground,
our features soft in the pale light
and simply human.

We planted bulbs where his ashes lay
and the mouths of the choir fell open
but no sound was coming out

and he having laid all deafness aside
must've heard on the wind
what our silence sang about.

No one will forget his eyes
or how wide his ears were.
It didn't rain to make the Bible wet

and I was close enough to hear
that in the beginning was the Word
and the wind was helping to turn the pages.

Christmas Night

I'm shaking these crumbs Lord
out under the stars this Christmas night.

We should have been glad in candlelight
but it's a dour face you see now
under my paper hat.

Tonight Lord your Son we celebrate;
but this girl you gave into our care—
I've cared and failed. Not at my table
can she break bread with grace.

I'm shaking Lord these crumbs out
Christmas night at the nerve end
of your starry agony.

Now you must father her, and midnight
be a touch of Mary upon her face.

The Lights and Shades

It's all green in the heights of Summer.
Please don't die. Please stay, here
where the lights and shades co-
operate in a breeze from nowhere.

·

Don't die. There's
not enough time. Not
now when the chives
sway tall and thin
and the things all
Winter hidden
are green again.

·

Why should you
on this Summer's day
when bees
shake the honeysuckle
why
when even the stones
are warmed
to their cold hearts
should you
why should you
want to die?

·

I wanted to be entirely light.
I wanted to be entirely
dark and beautiful
with my grapes and curls.
I wanted Paradise I suppose
and thought any moment
the world could turn a cheek
untroubled by any weakness.

·

Here amid the mingling
of the lights and shades
we stray, we ragged immortals.

Wishing and Wishing

These faces. Will soon be gone.
But the grass remains
moving its slender shadows
for other eyes, or for no eyes,
and not caring.
I can hear voices from over there
and now I cannot hear them.
Goodbye goodbye everything says,
each wave of the grass
each glance given.
We are here among stones and ferns
but the moment's nowhere.
I wish I wish is the sound
that the wind makes,
wishing and wishing.
I wish we were children again
all ferns and buttercups
and the grass unmown
before ever a passion shook us.
To be held from all harm.
Why should I brush my hair
if I don't want to.

4

The Long Grass of Childhood

The Memories that Belong to Fields

Grass. And sky. And a green river. I am afraid of cows.
Maybe there's a kite up there, trembling against the azure.

Such grass you could hide in. Such grass the picknickers flatten with a white cloth spread with orange juice and tomato sandwiches that have a lot of salt in them.

What if.

What if some theology students walked past.
But the God involved refuses to be talked about.

He prefers the orange juice.

He prefers the boats gliding in under the willows where the couples kiss then paddle out again.

I do not remember this.

But I remember this—that we set up a tent here then had to run home to get some butter.

Afraid of sheep too. But that was another time.

But.

But this field seems open so why not let them come—the memories that belong to fields, that float in the mist above them, above the river, above the water-snakes.

Just here I saw the naked man. And a bridge so thin it plunges me into the swan's reflection.

The Kingdom that I Left Behind

There was a river with swans.
That's all. Now that they've flown
I can reflect upon a white reflection.

On their pure whiteness I can reflect;
Or, in a moment when I least expect,
They'll glide into the mind serene and perfect.

And indeed forever they glide in the mind
Perfect and unkind
Back there in the kingdom that I left behind.

In the kingdom of my childhood
The river in flood
Carried a fierce perfection I never understood.

I never could understand the savage grace
Of swans reflecting on the water's face.

The Long Grass of Childhood

To be lost in the springtime fields
is to find yourself
in a place called Maybe-The-Wind-
Still-Shakes-The-Long-Grass-Of-Childhood.

We had grandmothers then.
Blue sky was a house for us.
The powder on a butterfly's wing
said who are you to be looking.

It is a place called Colour-
Can-Hurt-The-Heart. Who am I
in this field so vast no
grandmother could ever find me.

Seeing the Grass Green

There's a girl running with boots on.
Here's a me watching with eyes.

There is the grass green and seen.
Here is me seeing the grass green.

Trees—so treeful.
Me so meful.

What does it mean to be green and a tree?
What does it mean to me to be me?

Frog Song

The frog cannot sing very well
but he keeps on practising.

He can hop, though, and splash.
He dwells in a green silence.

The frog has no shoes at all
but wears elegant gloves.

Oh sing me a sweet frog song
deep down and cool.

I wish I could dwell like him
in that green silence.

Musical Bones

Marc Chagall's green uncle
practised the violin of his own body.

Even his bones were musical,
and every time he breathed
they fluted joyously.

He sang to the donkeys.

On moonlit nights
he danced on the rooftops
to his own heart-thumping accompaniment.

Chagall's uncle is dead now.
If anyone dug him up
not a tooth would they find,
but the white keys of a piano.

The Wild Tibetan Donkey

Hello, God! It's me!
Your wild Tibetan Donkey.
I've only got time
to stop and sing one psalm
and then I'll be off again
chasing my wild shadow.

'Accept neither pack nor saddle'—
that's what you told me.
Now tell me this—
how do your humans hear you
having such small ears?
I think you are the burden
men must carry.

I thank you, God,
that I'm not any beast of burden.
I can hullaballoo in the foothills
all I want; and if it shakes
the equilibrium of your prayerwheels
you have only yourself to blame.
Hee-Haw!
May it please you to find acceptable
my raucous song.

Whatever everlasting rest
you're preparing for me
forget it at once.
Even on that highest peak
I reckon to be dancing.

There is something
that you can do, though—
teach the chasms to bray,
teach even the mountains
to gallop on the last day.

The Pig (for Plato)

Pigs are philosophers.
That's why their tails
are curled as a question-mark.

Have you not heard them
grunting agreement
about the difficult works
of Bacon?

They can chew for hours
over Aristotle's *Poetics*,

or rootle in the woods
for new *Republics*
where poets
are not to be admitted perhaps
but certainly pigs are.

Oh no one disgruntles the pig.

Mud is meaning. That's
what a pig says.
We are what we eat.

And they grow quite
pink at the snort of it.

Some Words For You, Basho

I too can hear water,
but not the sound
of frogs jumping into the water.

The water I hear is not as old
as the one you heard
now and then being jumped into.

Now is not then—
but it is *late March*
and there is *a pigeon cooing*

and on a day like today
you heard
what's to be heard in water:

. . . . *a pond* . . . .
. . . . *a frog* . . . .
. . . . *and a splash* . . . .

Oh I could have written that!
So why do the circles spread
so wide from your frog's jumping?

There is no such thing as a water.
There is only water—a splashing
where now is then.

As your frog jumps now
and now into the sound of itself
I listen to my listening.

Paths of Silver

Today (the way you did, Basho)
I took to the road with my disciples

—one umbrella between us, the rain
streaming down, and not a thought
about the paths being slippery.

Half a day's journey
we came to an iron grate
set into the ground in front of us.

Nothing but Earth down there.

But on the brick sides of the shaft
five snails were clustered together
in a slow passion.

You would have liked that moment.

Little snails   (you would have said)
You too walk on paths of silver.

With Leonardo's Eyes

(You should look at certain walls stained with damp . . .)

Leonardo would have loved
      this garden wall
where the faces
      of nothing at all
move among ivies.

·

When Leonardo and I
      look through the same eyes
the shadows of ivy moving
      grow wilder than any form
ever walled in a garden.

·

My shadow splashed on the wall
      is all mossed and ivied.
I have seen gardens there
      to rival the bright leaves
of Leonardo's notebook.

·

Sunlight on this garden wall
      seems far
from any wars, Leonardo.
      Yet even here there are captains
mustering the ivy shadows.

·

To move through the garden
      with Leonardo's eyes
is to find
      all the Smiles you wish for
in the Louvre of ivy.

What Catrin Said

We had over 500 gardens in our roses this year,
I mean . . . . .

I mean each rose opened into 500 identical gardens
and in each one walked myself.

500 identical selves   each one a rose   each rose
a garden where I walked I mean.

This year   500 years   each year a garden.

The Walnut Shadow

This morning a drop of rain fell on my hand.

The roses were in full bloom, and the lions
were roaring louder than last Tuesday.

I began to sing—a song to touch the heart
of any child.

I stood for a moment lost in the Walnut shadow
and sang it again more quietly.

In the meadow beyond, the wild roses all
leaned and listened.

Even the lions stopped their noise
until that song was over.

The Nightingwolf

Keep far from yourself the Nightingwolf;
    she sings and devours.
The beauty of her one wild note
    withers the flowers.

Oh never avail the Wolfingale
    to unfurl his wings.
The teeth of his smile in the Linden tree
    have worried the roots of things.

Crimson

Cast down in sleep
beside a withering tree
I dream sometimes
of a bridge where Crimson
crossing to this world of shades
treads so close upon my heart
that I, half-waking,
cry at the sight
of her burning sandal

Poem for King David

You breathe in as kingdom

You breathe out as air

Your kingdom is everywhere

(These words came to me in sleep so I cannot be sure how the word 'air' should be spelt. 'Aire' is another possibility, for David sang to the harp. 'Heir' might also have been intended.)

Merlin's Song

Bring me a blade of grass
from King Arthur's grave,
and I'll whistle between my thumbs
a ditty that Merlin made
about a time to come
when his glamour would rise again
out of the trembling grasses.
This song he made for Vivaine.

Oh bring me a daisy flower
and let me upon the petals tell
whether she loves me loves me not.
No matter. In a simple hour
she crowned me with a daisy chain.
This song he made for Vivaine.

In the Grass this Morning

Beloved, the alphabet
glistens clean and new
in the fields this morning.

The grass on which we walk
is wet with another lifetime.

·

Beloved, you must own the footprints
though the shoes be borrowed.

I think the earth
which clings to them now
is not easily shaken.

·

Beloved, your lips moisten
as if an aire of Summer
said you
could be its Winter instrument.

·

Beloved, the gates and stiles
open a field where your beauty
always awaited me.

This crown upon my head—
I found it in the grass this morning.

The Hazel Shade

Hazel is the poet’s tree.
        All afternoon
I laboured in its shade,
        turning the earth over
to bring song back to the garden.

·

So long as Lucifer’s song
        hovered above the tree
my eyes were so dazzled
        they could see nothing original
in the humble shade of the Hazel.

·

All afternoon
        I laboured for original song,
but only when I gave
        my fame to the Hazel shade
did the true song come.

Hearts upon Paths

There are paths and
there are hearts.
Hearts upon paths.
Does a sideways glance
tumble a heart
into paths of chance?

There are eyes and
there are hearts.
Hearts stumble upon
eyes half
hidden in the grass.

The World's Wood

When the blind girls walk in the wood
the mouths of the stones say watch your step;
the wind takes care of them.

When the blind girls stop
they listen for the paths that say
this is the way that the good girls find
walking blind in the world's wood.

When the blind girls grope
to the topmost stair of the night
they climb another which isn't there
and tumble into brightness.

The Path of the Poets

The path of the poets has three stiles to cross
and an end uncertain:

at the first stile they blindfold you,
at the second stile you lose all sense of the way,
at the third stile you enter a new country.

The guardians of the path provide
a dark woman on your left
to guard you at all times,
a bright woman on your right to guide you;
but she only takes your hand
after the first field is crossed.

The path of the poets is without words.
You must speak with bird-tongues.
After the second stile the woodpecker
begins to work inside you.

And when you reach the third stile
they'll turn you round and around.
Let go let go and give yourself
into the hands of women.

The path of the poets is strewn with beechnuts
that suddenly roll from under you, and a magpie
screams at you from a hidden driveway.

Your name could make you blush. If anyone comes
the women press you against the hedge and hide you.

On the path of the poets the rain sounds lonelier;
and in the bluebell wood beyond arriving
they will untie your eyes
and drop the poem in your lap at last.

5

In Yielding

Hold the Evening Back

Move slowly gondola
and hold the evening back.

Move over Doge-wed waters
into that broad lagoon

where the ageless domes reflect
and the waves lap marble.

Move beyond wharves and words,
beyond every ache and lack.

But slowly slowly gondola.
Hold the evening back.

Bella Donna

Bella Donna, now that all other
loves of my youth subside
it's you I turn to

and in turning find
that your eyes have ever been
watchful over me

in the shade of night
in the midnight glimmer of a leaf
waiting for my return.

Whatever beauty I held
I render back now.
Whatever my eyesight

laid a claim to
I relinquish to your care.
I would have drowned

in the mirrors, Lady,
except that beyond all images
you waited there.

In Yielding

For the word 'yield'
      (which   in the form
            of an invisible flower
you gave me   and for which
      bending to accept
            without suspicion
I found a buttonhole)
      thanks. Believe me
            it is a gift
with seeds in it
      for future flowering.
            Break up the field
this Winter
      and let them fall
            invisible to invisible
into the heart's ground.
      The stars
            worm secrets there.
Frost and fire
      strip from the pulses
            whatever is not
the Nothing   which
      (yielding)
            yields a fieldful
of that flower you gave me.

Winter Crucifix

The dark square of this window,
the small circle of light
that my lamp casts on the table
are enough to make a world with.

The dark—it goes on and on.
Small light restore
the boundaries of my self to me.

Soldiers in the square
are battering at the doors.
Dear light secure
the circle of my certainty.

The dark dice of my window
are rattling without stars.
Dear light in the void
weave a seamless garment around me.

Rumours of the Word

Who came
    closer to Christ—
Thomas or John?

The one who
    listening at the heart
overheard
    rumours of the Word
before words began?

Or Thomas the doubter
    who touched
where the blood ran?

Christ—he loved
    John the best.
Yet Thomas who pressed
    his thumb
where the nails had stood

might claim
    through the pain he shared
as close a brotherhood.

Thorn Song

Did I choose this?

I dared to be chosen and said
Teach me what the North Wind
sighs to the thorn.

I dared to be born
under the pretty Rose-Tree.

She said *Open your heart*
to every passing song.

I opened to a song . . .
sharp as a thorn.

Ah but I chose it freely,
and what the wind sighed
I sing now.

Surely out of joy it springs.

Go, My Songs

Go, my songs, and beg
forgiveness from the ones
you brought into confusion.

If any girl admired
your glittering syllables
confess that they deceived her.

If any lip grew moist
say promiscuity
is a music's best behaviour,

professing sincerity
in a thousand mouths at once,
whistled by everyone.

Go, my songs. The air
upon the open field
is reft of melody.

Ode for Woden

Neglecting now to sound
their lovely syllables
we have turned Elm to lament
Ash Oak into a broken syntax.

We have soured the Saxons' ground.

Their syllable could stand
closer up to a thing,
probing through the knotted grain
to where the Un-thing stood.

Crashing among the boughs
folk heard   Woden himself
giddy with rune-making.

That was long ago.

We with our sour rain
have stripped rune from leaf
leaving it bereft
of what could best sustain it.

Elm. Ash. Oak. For love of these
I'm overwhelmed,   ashamed
to leave their Names unspoken.

Poet to Painter

(for Christian von Grumbkow)

Am I permitted to say
what I see in your painting, Sir?
Or does its significant fire
transcend what a word can weigh?

I've tried not to conceptualize
the turmoils of your canvas,
but it hurts to withhold the focus
craved by my conventional eyes.

Yet, if I could risk bewilderment
and hold myself trembling here
I think I might breathe the air
which moved before the event

of putting paint upon whiteness.
Your colours (before they signify)
ask my devoted eye
to be no more than a witness

to their deeds and sufferings.
Your blues and yellows and reds
bend now to be interpreted—
but they rage at the heart of things.

And you have the heart, I say,
to accompany them in your blood
and come to what I never understood
having only my words to weigh.

The Groundless Ground

Dear Mr Turner,

you know your painting of the steam-boat in a snowstorm? Well, I gave a talk about it the other day in front of a hundred people.

Already in your lifetime people were talking. Not always kindly. *All soapsuds and whitewash,* one called it. And, *Before any further account of the vessel can be given it will be necessary to wait until the storm has cleared off a little.*

But the storm never did clear, did it! And by the time the 20th century arrived everything was in motion, no boat anywhere in sight, watcher and watched tossed together upon the canvas.

But when a more recent critic calls it a demonstration of the *puniness of Man's creation in the face of the forces of nature,* I remember with what pride you wrote: *I got the sailors to lash me to the mast to observe it.*

I did not paint it to be understood, you said. *No one had any business to like the picture.* Call it a strength, rather, but one not to be understood by the detached observer.

The participator however (beyond like and dislike) moves into those rhythms of the sea and snow and steam and fire from the signals sent out, and stands with you at the mast, scientist and artist in one, holding a centre amid the elements—a certainty of being, a human dignity founded upon nothing but its own inner ground.

When I gave the talk about your painting I tried to demonstrate that gesture by balancing a wooden rod on one finger, showing how all outer motion slowly dies away and moves to a still point maintained only so long as I am active and present to confirm it.

It was hard to do it, though, with those hundred pairs of eyes upon me, and my hand did shake a little.

I showed also how, having found that stillness, we can walk and carry it freely into the world, holding, as you did (*on the night 'The Ariel' left Harwich*) a creative direction through wild water.

The Ariel . . . your century wanted something solider. But in mine that least substantial thing is our only surety, and I say with you—*I do not expect to escape, but feel bound to record it if I do so.*

Eadfrith's Lullaby

Round Lindisfarne the waves are pages.
Blues once used by the saints and scribes
Roll now upon the agnostic tides.

Tonight upon the North Sea rolls
A yearning for those glittering scrolls
That spoke of a Spirit upon the water.

Upon these waters God still broods
And the lonely seagulls wheel and cry
That once were Eadfrith's lullaby.

Eadfrith loved the clamorous birds
And blessed them. In his breast they stirred
A Gospel he alone could bear.

When the tides informed his naked heart
That the blues and fires upon his pen
Could inscribe a word entirely human

He wound their waves into God's own Name
Till on the glittering page there flamed
Nature and Maker woven in one.

Biographical Note

Paul Matthews (b. 1944) works as a poet and gymnast at Emerson College, in Forest Row, Sussex. In the late 60s he edited with Paul Evans the poetry magazine, *Eleventh Finger,* making contact with many of the leading poets in America (including Robert Duncan, who has been a particular inspiration for his work). He has travelled widely, reading from his poetry, and offering courses in Creative Writing based upon his book, *Sing Me The Creation* (Hawthorn Press). He has also edited an anthology of contemporary poetry, *With My Heart In My Mouth* (Rudolf Steiner Press).

In *The Ground That Love Seeks,* Paul Matthews presents new work together with poems that have appeared over many years in a wide range of magazines, booklets and anthologies.